A Mind 4 Cricket

RAISE YOUR GAME WITH
MENTAL TRAINING

Paul Maher

authorHOUSE®

AuthorHouse™ UK Ltd.
500 Avebury Boulevard
Central Milton Keynes, MK9 2BE
www.authorhouse.co.uk
Phone: 08001974150

This book is a work of non-fiction. Unless otherwise noted, the author and the publisher make no explicit guarantees as to the accuracy of the information contained in this book and in some cases, names of people and places have been altered to protect their privacy.

First published by AuthorHouse 9/3/2008

ISBN: 978-1-4343-9789-8 (sc)

Neither PAUL MAHER or MIND 4 PUBLICATIONS will be held responsible for any accident or misadventure arising from the improper use of information laid out in this manual. This manual is written specifically for someone to learn self-hypnosis, not as tuition to hypnotise others.

Printed in the United States of America
Bloomington, Indiana

This book is printed on acid-free paper.

Attention

The information here is intended for people in good health. The ideas, suggestions and techniques here are not a substitute for proper medical advice. Anyone with medical problems of any kind should consult a medical practitioner. Any application of the ideas, suggestions or techniques here are at the readers sole discretion.

This publication contains the authors opinion in the subject matter covered herein. The author makes no warrantry of any kind for any particular purpose. The author is not liable or responsible to any person or entity for any consequential, incidental or special damage caused or alleged to be caused directly or indirectly for the information contained within.

Registration entitles you to any future e-book updates, bonus report updates. Electronic books, known as e-books are protected worldwide under international copyright and intellectual property law, the same as printed books, recorded material and other literary works.

Table of Contents

Introduction

> *"Our fascination with cricket is that it never ceases to fascinate."*
>
> - David Rayvern Allen

Welcome. I want to share with you techniques that will motivate you to success in your sport, teach you strategies that have helped many cricketers break through their limitations and control your thinking, so you can play the game others dream.

Throw away any limitations forever, the quality of your game will catapult you to new heights, after all, the achievements of one player can energise and inspire their whole team.

Cricket is a great game to grow and evolve. Remember as a child the excitement of unwrapping your first cricket bat? It wont take long to read this manual, but the techniques you learn will serve you in your career and beyond. Your playing career can be over before you know it, you owe it to yourself to have a stormer.

Let me answer that question going on in your mind…what's it all about? Mental skills and Sport Psychology are not modern concepts, they've been around for as long as sports have been played and are as much about mental attitude as solid technique. It now plays an increasing role in shaping a players performance. NLP emerged about thirty years ago as a way to identify how people regulate their behaviours unconsciously and if required, re-programme their mind. Handy techniques taught here guide you toward powerful, positive change. Your mind is the most important body part you can train, here I'll show you how to reach your full potential.

If your cynical, believe learning is boring, think this is all weird new-age stuff, we need to have a chat. It does work. Hundreds of therapists like myself and thousands of clients say it does work. There are poor therapists about, so if you or a colleague have tried something like this before and failed, get over it! Sorry to be so blunt, but doom mongers and nayers will never become better Cricketers.

As a human, you have an incredible mind that can sometimes get wired up in a way that is not useful for some situations you find yourself in. The unconscious acts in a literal, even naïve way. As it's non-judgemental, it will absorb a bad idea as much as a good one. Culture, family, peer pressure, a bad coach, all teach ways that sometimes just aren't useful for what you want to achieve.

This manual is just like having me sit down with you and go over, step-by-step, exactly how to do the techniques. The goal of this manual is to help you get greater control of yourself and cricket by planting positive suggestions in your mind. The secret to successful Cricket is very simple. Do something…anything at all! Even if you mess up you'll be wiser for the experience. You have to take action, that's what separates winners from losers.

Use this manual as an interactive tool to challenge, excite, inspire and teach. Don't underestimate the methods, you can find them invaluable. If you consider a technique you find

strange or not to your liking, simply find another that you can adjust to suit your need, there will be a more exciting one for you on another page. Allow yourself some quiet space and time to go

through these techniques properly. It can all start with one technique and it will start by knowing that technique well. Don't attempt to go all out to learn them all right away. Learn one then extend your range. Even the simple act of doing a minor one can get you moving onto others.

I have made examples of situations, but your free to use them as a template which can be adapted to suit your needs. They are not quick fix miracle cures, you have to put the time in to learn and use them, but the successful methods you are about to learn will help you begin making a wave of changes, now, on this first day. Chances are you'll be bitten by the bug as you find your confidence grow. Excited? You should be. These methods can rock you to your core. These methods can also affect other areas of your life. Just sit back, put your feet up and enjoy what I am going to teach you. It starts here...

What About You?

Your behaviour is a result of your self-image, the person you believe you really are. Your self-image is so strong your behaviour will have you perform consistently as the person you think you are.

We all know people who are skilled, yet think they're not. They're too fat, too slow, too old, too out of shape, whatever. If you believe that about yourself, if you believe yourself not good enough in any way, you will unconsciously sabotage any effort to make yourself a winner. Batting too defensively only creates confidence in the bowler.

Studies have proven time after time, an extraordinary number of sportspeople fail because they think themselves less than they are worth through this limited self-image. Are they unworthy? Of course not. It's how they see themselves in their imagination which affects their performance and can even causes self-destructive behaviour.

Here's an example to prove my point. Sit for a moment somewhere quiet and remember some time in the past when you felt tired, sad, despondent. Really get back into that time by remembering everything you could see and hear in as much detail as you can. Bring back any physical and emotional experiences, get that memory and hold it for a few seconds. Try to stand up.

Now sit down again and this time bring back to mind a time when you felt energetic, determined, optimistic. Again remember in as much vivid detail as you can, what you saw, hear the good things you heard and get in touch with the physical and emotional feelings you had and hold them for several seconds. Now stand up.

Compare the two experiences. In the first you may have found it an effort to stand. How about the second? Did you leap up, ready to go? Your thoughts influence how you perform. Isn't it interesting that in just a few seconds, thinking one way then another created an entirely different result. Your belief about yourself influences your thoughts which then affect your behaviour, as this manual will prove.

That said, let me remind you how quickly your cricketing career goes by. For instance, it's incredible how the last twelve months have gone by. How was it? Think about your mortality. Imagine your breathing your last. Did you do all you wanted to do in Cricket? Did you truly live it? Visit the venues you always wanted? Enjoy wonderful moments with your team mates? Before you know it, you find yourself retired, then into old age and here you are, staring into emptiness, reflecting on how good you could have been. That's how it ends up for the vast majority of people. Where did all the time go?

The only thing you have total control of in this world is your thinking. At first you may feel self-conscious trying out these methods. Whenever you do something new that takes you beyond your 'comfort zone' you feel nervous. It's OK, your human. You must grit your teeth and get out of your 'comfort zone'. Be task-conscious not self-conscious.

This manual will open up to you clear ideas as to what you need to do to create the future you want. Nothing in your life is going to change unless you change. You are fully capable of mental and physical feats. You are bigger than you think, capable of more than you can imagine.

Your in the process of thinking with belief…

Belief

" *Man is what he believes.* **"**

— Anton Chekhov

You're the opening batsman. You need concentration, courage and self-control to blunt the onslaught of an aggressive fast bowler looking for blood. There's a new ball and you may face a close, attacking field. Belief gives you the assurance to trust in your ability.

Belief dominates behaviour whether positively or negatively and behaviour affects performance. Your physical behaviour is controlled by belief. A belief is knowing with absolute certainty what something means. That belief can mean the difference between an ordinary player and a world conqueror. Success or failure. You always prove yourself right. However, a lower order batsman with a good technique can improve with the desire belief can bring.

In other way's belief can determine your quality of happiness, health, wealth and success. It even has a greater influence on your life than the actual truth.

Notice the successful players. They've made more mistakes than those who haven't. Every mistake has been used as a learning opportunity for them. They continued to believe in themselves. Failure is part of the learning process, not the end of it. It's only a frustration.

When have you failed? Only when you stopped believing. Every response was information to tell you what action's were getting you closer to, or further away from what you wanted.

We all get stuck in our beliefs, however sensible we think they are. You may find it interesting that you tend to believe what you think is true, without questioning. If you believe you can't spin bowl, it's because you believe you can't spin bowl. But the interesting thing is, if you tell yourself you can, that then gives you permission to question that defeatist belief and soon, with consistent practice, you will find that you can spin bowl-can't you! What you believe isn't necessary real, you just have to invest in yourself. Confused? The nice thing about being confused is you come out of it with something new.

Belief creates self-talk, how you speak to yourself inside your head. If your going to say something to yourself, you may as well make it something good.

Take a belief which is holding you back.
Think about or write down it's opposite, more positive belief.
Imagine what it would be like living this new belief?
Believe that:
You do have the ability to succeed.
You can accomplish anything.
There are no problems, just opportunities.
Your creating your future now
If you begin to believe your destined to be a successful Cricketer, you will be.

Now that kind of thinking can give you a buzz you wont believe!

And the openers? Most openers bide their time, playing the patience game, gauging the behaviour of the pitch, the pace of the bowlers, going onto the back foot and taking low-risk shots. However, some will believe the ball is there to be hit and assert their authority from the start, confident in the face of the bowlers hostility.

Believe in the power of your imagination...

Imagination

"You can't build a reputation on what your going to do. It's simple, fantasize, rehearse, then go out into the world and do it!"

- Henry Ford

Imagine that I've just cut a lemon in two and I've handed you one of the halves. Notice it's texture there in your hand as you bring it up to your mouth. Be aware of the citric smell while you place the juicy fruit in your mouth. Now suck on all that tangy lemon juice and let it run down your throat.

As your reading this, imagine both of your hands are submerged in a bucket of hot, soapy water. You can remember what that's like? Did you have a bath last night, wash the windows, or even your car? Recall that feeling of hot soapy water on your hands, make it vivid, feel those pinpricks of watery heat.

Your unconscious mind can't tell the difference between a real, or imagined event, it's just like a VCR. It records sights and sounds continuously. Your body then treats every vivid thought and image as if it was real. Ever awakened from a nightmare? Notice how your body responds to the vivid use of your imagination more so than a conscious command. If you order your

9

heart to speed up, it probably wont. If you imagine in detail walking down a dark sinister alley, late at night and hear fast, approaching footsteps behind you, I bet your heartbeat will increase. What about that nightmare? It wasn't real but you woke up in a sweat, your heart pounding, gripped with fear and it took a while for you to calm down.

Everyone has the ability to imagine, I may have proven it to you. If not, answer these questions:

Think of your locker in the changing room. What does it look like? Where is the door handle? What sound does it make when you shut it? To answer you had to use your imagination.

Now by changing the pictures and sounds in your mind, you can gain conscious control of any aspect of your game. Images that are bigger, brighter, bolder have a greater impact than those which are smaller, duller and further away. Let me show you.

Think of someone you found stressful to play against or who rankled you. Think about facing them again. A bad memory can hurt you like a knife. They can beat you without a ball being bowled. Here's something your going to love. Recall their face. As you do so, ask yourself:

Is the memory in colour or black and white?
Is their face in your memory to the left, to the right, or there, right in front of you?
Is it large or small?
Is it light or dark?
Moving or still?
Are there any sounds?

Now play around with the way you are remembering that person. Make each of these changes in turn and notice what happens:

If the memory has colour, drain it all away until it is like a black and white photo.

Move the position of the image and push it further away from you.

Shrink it down in size.

Turn down the brightness, make it fuzzy.

If the image is moving, freeze frame it.

What sound do you hear? Is it their voice? Change it by giving them a squeaky voice like a cartoon character, or a deep sexy one, go on, do it.

Finally, give the face a clown's nose, bright orange or green hair, Mickey Mouse ears. Go on, have fun!

Altering your memory can change how you feel. Think of the person again in this new way. How do you feel? Probably the stressful memory has diminished if not gone completely. Not only do you feel different now, imagine how comfortable you will feel the next time you face that person. It's your control, your emotions, your thinking which belongs to you, not someone controlling you.

Let me show you how to use imagination in a way known as association and dissociation. Think of another stressful or uncomfortable memory. Keep that image in your mind, now step out of yourself so you can see the back of your head. I know you may be sceptical, at least give me a hearing. Now move away as far from the situation as you can. Step all the way out of the picture so you can still see it, but way over there somewhere as if it's happening to someone else. Shrink it down. Lose all the colour. Turn the background fuzzy or white. Fade away any sound. Notice by dissociating reduces the intensity of the feelings you were having. It takes courage to learn new skills such as these.

You can do the same to heighten a good memory, by association. When you think about happy memories, you re-create the happy feelings associated with them. If you were to remember a time when you felt really confident, aware of your ability, strength and self-belief. Now let the image come into your mind, make it juicy. Step into that memory as if your there again, seeing through your own eyes, hearing through your ears and feeling how successful you felt in your body. Enlarge the memory, make it bigger and brighter, the feelings stronger, turn up the sounds and make them richer. If you can't remember a time, imagine how it would feel to be totally confident. You get what you focus on.

To reduce a negative memory, step out, move away from it (dissociate). Watch it as if it's happening to someone else, shrink it, turn it black & white, dull, out of focus. Make the sounds quieter, further away. Doing this can cause any bad emotional response to drain away. Notice your controlling how it affects you.

To improve a positive memory, zoom in and fully experience it (associate). Make the image bigger and closer, intensify the colour, increase the brightness, make the sounds closer, louder, unless it's a memory of peace and quiet. Live it. You can have a great deal of fun with these methods.

Imagine your batting. Step into a picture of yourself controlling the ball, hitting fours and sixes almost at will. Feel mighty and proud. Hear the 'thunk' of every perfectly hit ball. Notice the fielders. Slip catchers, a gully, a short leg. Shrink them down and turn them into black and white, move them further away from you, duller, quieter. The bowler unable to penetrate or establish any rhythm. Now do the same as a bowler, go on, I'm not going to do everything for you.

You can use your imagination to free yourself of any old, negative beliefs that might be limiting you. That's right! Imagine them written or painted on a wall. Gripping a bat in your hands, attack the wall, demolish it completely, see the dust, hear the noise of bricks tumbling, feel the energy your using until the words or images are totally destroyed.

You could imagine them drawn or written on paper. Feel the paper between your hands as you rip it to shreds, hear it, feel it, see it happen there in your minds eye. Finish off by ritually burning it. I said some methods would challenge you-this is all revolutionary stuff!

Here's an easier one. Close your eyes and imagine in your mind a picture of the player you wish to become. See how you will be dressed, your balanced stance, the expression on your face, all the tiny details. Take that picture and throw it up into the air and multiply it so that hundreds of copies come raining down all around you as far as your eye can see. They even go into your past and your future.

Did that feel awkward? Exercises like these may seem silly, but while you control the pictures in your mind and how they sound, your not at the mercy of anyone else or circumstance and they direct your unconscious mind toward being the cricketer you want. A flame will ignite inside you.

I'll teach you next about self-talk...

Self-Talk

" My life has been full of terrible misfor-
tunes, most of which never happened. "

- Michel de Montaigne

Also known as internal dialogue, self-talk is simply the way
you talk to yourself inside your head. You worry over a bad
innings, congratulate yourself after a good result, even tell
yourself how sexy you look in fresh, clean whites. People do
it every day, but mostly it's negative. Blaming yourself, chas-
tising yourself. 'I'm not good enough,' 'I'm too tired,' 'I'm
not able.' This is one of the major causes of poor performance. If you tell yourself something often enough, you'll
begin to believe it. It may not be true, but you will certainly
believe it is. If you have negative beliefs, you have negative
self-talk which will confirm the negative belief and so it goes
on. You must be aware of your internal dialogue. While
positive thinking may not always work, negative thinking
almost always does. Put aside any self-pity and accept the
responsibility to change. If the voice you use isn't supporting you, change it.

A major problem for sports people is the repeated dwelling
over poor performance. This memory leads to negative self-

talk along with emotional discomfort. Your mind may then remember similar bad events. Allowing the past to affect you instead of focusing on the present only slows you down. You suffer tight muscles, energy loss, poor coordination which all add to the bad performance. Future chapters will show you the techniques to use to get over these poor memories.

Be good to yourself when you talk to yourself by talking positively. Make mental pictures of yourself being a total success. See yourself taking those wickets, hear the congratulations of your team mates and the applause from the spectators and feel how good you feel when you practice being a winner. Mental rehearsal is the next best thing to actually being successful, so do it as often as you can and review it with positive self-talk. You'll be delighted when you see those improvements.

What do you say to yourself when things go wrong?
What do you say to yourself when confronted by a challenge?

The secret is a confident Cricketer will talk differently to himself than one who lacks that confidence, even though they perform equally well. Playing with confidence gives you the security to enjoy every minute and will be reflected by your game. Without that confidence another player may always feel unprepared, nervous, undecided. Those thoughts will then reinforce those beliefs. So you see how vital confident, positive self-talk is.

Self-talk after a good performance:

Confident cricketer	Cricketer lacking confidence
I am like that.	It was luck.
I always perform like that.	It was a one-off
I'll be the same next time.	I can't do that again.

Self-talk after a poor performance:

Confident cricketer	Cricketer lacking confidence
It was luck.	I am like that.
It was a one-off.	I always perform like that.
I can't do that again.	I'll be the same next time.

Are you holding yourself back through perfectionism…

Perfectionism

> *" "I don't care what you say about me, just*
> *spell my name right! "*

-P. T. Barnum

A perfectionist can get hung up on themselves doing things perfectly! They can be their own worst enemy because they are never satisfied with their performance. A self-critical perfectionist can never be perfect in their mind because of a fear of making mistakes. That is the greatest barrier to success. Beneath the desire to succeed and reach excellence, a perfectionist often has an ultra-negative, condemning dialogue going on inside their head.

Yes, a perfectionist hates to lose, but a perfectionist must not get anxious about losing.

Some psychologists believe perfectionists are that way due to conditional parenting. The child's role in life has already been decided. Rarely satisfied parents who want their offspring to be a sporting success have no idea what they are doing to their child's self-esteem with their critical comments. When they criticise, they are telling their child, or so the child believes, s/he is a failure in their parents eyes. Children are easily influenced and will develop that fear of failure which can affect them unconsciously for years to come.

So, when you do well, do you give yourself enough credit? When you do poorly do you beat yourself up? Do you punish yourself if you make a mistake? If you gang up on yourself there are now two people fighting you. All Cricketers experience failure at some stage, it's how you emotionally handle it that determines if you leave it in the past or re-create it over and over.

Perfectionism damages excellence. Perfectionism doesn't exist, excellence does. Focus on the things you can control. Put errors behind you, loosen the stays on your self criticism-let it go! Don't get angry with yourself, move on. Concentrate on what's happening right in front of you, in the present, forget what's just happened, it's history.

A perfect Cricketer is optimistic, do you think he criticises himself…

The Inner Critic

―――――――――――――――――――――――――――――――――――

> *" We don't see things as they are, but rather*
> *as we are. "*
>
> - Anais Nin

Everybody's a critic and the worst you will ever come across is the one inside your head. This talk has a detrimental effect on your emotional state, even worse than someone in the crowd screaming at you. What does it sound like? Is it angry, sarcastic, resigned? When you make a mistake I bet you never say 'good, that's another learning experience.'

People think because there is a voice inside their head, they must listen to it. You can choose.

Criticism should be constructive if it's going to be of use. If your critical self-talk is not supporting you, play with the direction and tone of the voice. Like many of the methods presented in this manual, this one may seem strange at first. Go give it a shot, you have nothing to lose and everything to gain if it works. Is that reasonable?

The scoreboard isn't ticking over, your hemmed in by close fielders. You berate yourself for uncertain footwork.

Notice your critical voice with that nasty tone.

Now notice where it is coming from, inside or outside your head? From the front, sides, or back?

If your right handed, extend your left arm, left handed, extend your right.

Stick out the thumb of the extended arm.

Wherever the critical voice came from, imagine you can move it away from your head to your shoulder, then to your elbow, to your wrist, now move it all the way down your arm to the very tip of your thumb.

Hear the voice repeat the same thing, only this time as if you hear the voice coming from the tip of your thumb. Slow it right down, or speed it up. Change it to be like Mickey Mouse, Donald Duck or another cartoon character. Change the tone to something comical.

Move the voice down to your big toe.

You can use another voice to make the negative one shut up.

This technique can also be used on bad memories of someone talking critically to you. You understand this, can you not?

I'll make an interesting comment about critical self-talk. It always takes a hold in the unconscious as a command. So if you tell yourself your going to make a bad catch, be run out, you may trip or bowl wide, then it will probably happen. This is because negative self-talk generally has a strong emotion attached to it. A positive suggestion, no matter how good the intention, is usually wishful thinking, it does not contain that emotional content.

If you want to change for the better, pay close attention to the words you use on yourself, they can change the way you perform. Power, timing and placement can get the scoreboard moving for you and when you repeat something with enough emotion, you start to believe it. Use words and phrases that will motivate you and fill you with enthusiasm for the game. Every sportsperson has two competing voices, one is the negative critic, the other a positive coach. Who you listen to is your choice.

Lets re-programme your self-image…

Re-programme Your Self-Image

> " *We are never deceived; we deceive our-selves.* "
>
> - Goethe

To alter any poor memories or attitudes you may have about your game, first weaken them then create better alternatives by using the methods outlined in this manual. Your able to go into activities and situations with an abundance of vigour and enthusiasm. Just give yourself time.

Clasp your hands in your usual way, fingers entwined and notice which thumb is on top. Let go then clasp your hands again in such a way as the opposite thumb is on top. How do you feel? Awkward? Uncomfortable? It doesn't feel natural! The further you go into unfamiliar territory, the greater the psychological discomfort. Your performance may suffer temporarily as you make needed adjustments to your game, but change does that. If you were to place your hands and thumb the 'awkward' way every time, it would eventually feel natural, as your adjustments will.

You have talent. Can you adjust to a new team or league? This method will show you how to perform with confidence.

Take a deep breath, sit back and relax as you exhale.

Tighten, then relax all your muscle groups.

Recall the sights, sounds, feelings of you performing at your very best.

In your minds eye imagine another you standing in front of you. This is the best that you have ever been, or ever will be, at the top of your game, every decision you make is the right one.

If you can't see it or imagine it, just know that it's there.

When you feel happy with the image in front of you, notice the way you stand, move, hit, bowl, catch.

Notice a confident champion before you, bowling a good length ball every time, a unstoppable batsman or a superb wicketkeeper.

Now step into your image and see through those eyes, hear through those ears, and feel how good it feels to be that living image.

Keep that important feeling and make everything bigger, brighter, more powerful. Let it glow.

You can step into a more intense image of yourself. Do that several times, getting bigger and brighter and stronger each time.

Take a few minutes if you wish to imagine yourself in any situation from the past where you want a bad memory changed to a positive outcome, or see yourself in a future situation dominating play, being rewarded, excelling. You can, you know, forget about ever having had that problem.

Daydream and know it can come true.

Think of a future situation or event when having a positive feeling will be desired. Take tail-end batting. You've read the routine above, give it a go, or try this one next:

Using the Circle of Excellence exercise builds a positive mood and creates a state of mind which will be useful in that future.

In front of you, create a Circle of Excellence. This represents that state you require. Imagine it has a colour, maybe there is a sound there. This circle brings for you all the skills and positive assurance you want.

Now, return to a time when you had that positive resource or imagine you had the right attitude, dedication and grit.

Take a deep breath, exhale…

Step into the memory inside the circle.

Imagine the bright colour shinning down and all around going into every cell of your body, from the top of your head, all the way down to the tip of your toes. Double the brightness.

Tell yourself you are more confident, talented, fitter.

Every breath you take, you take in more of the resource, your demoralising the fielders.

Stop.

Take a step back, away from the circle and shake yourself off.

Choose a special word that will have meaning for you or a sound.

Again step into the circle and this time say or think the special word, hear that sound.

Imagine that feeling you have getting stronger, being absorbed by your body, strength and enthusiasm glows from you. Your more tenacious, hanging around the crease, your under no pressure, all your runs are a bonus to your team. If you can see it in your minds eye, you can achieve it.

You can do the Circle of Excellence just about anywhere. Rehearse first, then going onto the playing field, imagine the circle before you just before stepping onto the pitch. Do it as you take position at the wicket, before you turn to start your run to bowl. How about stepping out of the shower. Getting out of a car.

Feeling good? Your learning to master your emotions…

Master Your Emotions

> *"No matter how thin you slice it, there are always two sides."*
>
> - Baruch Spinoza

You keep coming back for more now, don't you. If you want to win the game going on inside your head, you have to deal with your emotions. I'm going to guide you to be your most confident self and feel resourceful in just a moment, for any endeavour you choose.

You may be wondering what is an emotion? An emotion is the mood you are in at any particular moment and is individual and unique to all of us. Love, hate, confidence, fear, they are all emotions and we constantly go in and out of them all day long. All behaviour is the result of an emotion.

Remember times when you were filled with confidence, determination, joy, optimism. Alas, you also suffered anger, depression and fear. Emotions are your unconscious minds way of telling you there is something going on you should pay attention too.

Here you'll learn how to programme yourself to experience more of the resourceful emotions you want in all the situations you want. The pictures you make in your imagination and the way you talk to yourself are known as internal representations. And that's all they are, representations, not real life, so they can't harm you.

Changes in breathing, muscle tension, posture, even facial expression all influence your feelings and behaviour, as you may now appreciate.

Think of a time when you felt nervous, anxious, defeated. Notice how it affects your posture, your shoulders slump and your head may have dropped.

I can show you a simple way to change. Wherever you are, plant your feet firmly on the ground, hold yourself tall, pull your shoulders back, take a great big breath, let it out, look up at the ceiling or the sky and put a great big grin on your face. Smile with your whole face with feeling. Now try to remember that tense situation again. Notice your mood has probably lifted and you no longer remember it in the same unpleasant way.

Why not keep the feeling there. Stand straight, let your spine support you while you imagine a bright golden thread running up your spine and straight out to the sky. Let yourself relax held up by this golden thread.

If your body is tense, it is producing different chemicals to when it is relaxed, so you feel and think differently. See how making physiological changes makes a difference to your emotional response.

And there's a lot said about pressure...

Pressure

Pressure gets a bad name. It's the ultimate lie detector. When it's present it can be a positive force bringing out the best in you, or a negative one, being an excuse to quit. Some Cricketers will break through, while those less committed break down. Everyone feels pressure in competition, no one is immune. It can often start long before the game begins. Cricketers under pressure become internally self-conscious rather than externally task-conscious. Worrying about making a mistake will usually get you one.

Recall a time when you felt pressure. Remember what you were doing, feeling, saying. Were you excited or nervous? Did you expect failure or feel a desire to win? Did you let all kinds of negative thoughts come into your mind?

Excessive mental pressure often produces mental blocks. Then anything recently learnt in training, be it technical or tactical may well be forgotten.

Become mentally tough, look at pressure as a challenge to drive yourself that much harder.

Pressure creates muscle tension, causing over-tightness, generally in the neck and shoulders. The heart beat goes up, breathing quickens, skin perspires. Some feel their stomachs churn.

When your tense, you want to get your task over as soon as possible. Mentally your mind races. The more you hurry, the worse you will probably play, making mistakes, creating even more pressure and greater muscle tension, so wasting more energy.

Interestingly, a way to relax tense muscles is first tighten them further. If your shoulders feel like coiled springs, slowly draw them up and squeeze them. Hold for fifteen seconds. Feel the sensation. Then release slowly and relax completely. Notice how they feel.

Days before an important game, a trial, appearing before selectors, a little nervousness may creep in. So actually the game begins before the game begins. At home, the journey to the venue, in the changing room. How do you reduce pressure and place your mind in the hear and now? Here's one method to give yourself an advantage. When you arrive in the changing room, use each article of clothing you remove, jacket or blazer, shirt, trousers, one shoe, then the another, to let go of a concern or irrational fear.

Each article of kit you put on, imagine your putting on resources of relaxation, courage or resilience. By the time you have changed, any distraction you were focused on will have dissolved. Now your in the right time zone and in the best state of mind for what's ahead.

Lets see how you can drive away the spectre of anger...

Anger & Psyching

> *"Learn to control your emotions or they will control you. "*
>
> *-Edgar Martinez*

Anger is born out of frustration and expectation. It feeds on itself. When you allow anger to get the best of you, it generally brings out the worst in you. Anger blocks concentration, tactics and technique. Your temper can hurt your team mates, they will find it difficult to trust you and you may despise yourself after for being so destructive.

You can let opponents or situations tie you up in knots. Your heart beats faster, your breathing quickens. Your stood there, all clenched jaw, staring eyes and hunched up shoulders and arms, hacked off and out of control. Or you can learn from it.

You control your moods and emotions. If someone makes you angry, your giving that person power over you. They are then controlling your moods and emotions.

Anger can often be fear in disguise as anger is based on insecurity. Non-violent fighting spirit is based on self-confidence.

Cricketers who cannot control their anger will never make great players. The best have the maturity to master their emotions, not to be servants to them. That emotional energy allows you to raise your game. Many sportspeople can channel anger positively as it motivates them. Anger kept under control will work for you.

Psyching or gamesmanship comes with the territory. Cheating, provocation, verbal abuse, lie's are all designed to upset you emotionally and disrupt your concentration. Recognise it for what it is and don't allow sledging to get inside your head and ruin your composure. If it affects you it's there, at the back of your mind. Even if you pretend it doesn't bother you, it does.

Be also aware there are two kinds of psyching-one your opponent does and the one you do to yourself. Come closer my friend. A way to divert anger is to divert your attention. Develop a ritual when you need to calm yourself or when you need a few moments to get yourself together. Pick a spot or a mark on the field or around the ground. Between each play walk to that mark and touch it, or if that's not possible, look at it. This strategy can keep your mind focused while you give yourself a pep talk.

Do something physical to slow events down for yourself. Rub your hands together, tie your laces, rub the bat, bounce the ball. Nothing too complicated. These are all small psychological boosts for mental and emotional management. When you can, change into a dry shirt, fresh socks, put on a sweat band. Do some small change to make things feel like it's a new start.

You could always do unto others what they do to you. Often they can't take it. Your now taking the initiative, however, do you really need to lower yourself to their level? The best response is be mature and have compassion for someone who has to resort to gamesmanship to defeat you as they can't do it through talent alone. Lets calm ourselves with breathing…

Breathing

Often overlooked, correct breathing should be carried out at all times, not only when you feel tense, as it calms your body and mind. When you breath normally, your body is unconsciously maintaining the balance of oxygen and carbon dioxide. When apprehensive, breathing changes to fast and shallow. This causes dizziness, poor vision, tiredness, breathlessness which only increases further anxiety.

If you practice correct breathing, it becomes second nature, so you must breath properly when your anxious, it will help keep you 'grounded'.

Most people breath into the chest area. Some breath into their abdomen, while a few breath into the area of the collar bone so they always seem to be gulping or gasping for breath. Where do you breath?

Lie on your back. Place one hand on your chest and the other on your abdomen. Breath out to empty your lungs. Now breath in your normal fashion. Don't force it as you may get light-headed in which case give it a rest till you feel better

Which hand rises and falls the most? Is it the one on your chest? Well your not breathing deeply enough. You should be breathing into your abdomen.

Here's how. Breath in through your nose and out through your mouth. Imagine a position an inch or two below your naval and your sending the breath you breath down to it. Your should feel your stomach area swell as you inhale. If it doesn't, place something light, like a paperback book on your abdomen and as you inhale, concentrate on making it rise.

When you breath into the chest you are only filling your lungs about three-quarters, the bottom quarter being stale air. Breathing into the abdomen actually fills all the lungs with fresh, rich air which can only do you good.

Oxygen is energy. It helps relax the muscles and clears the mind. When you hold your breath you create pressure and a nervous feeling develops. Slow, deep breathing will make you feel relaxed, keeping your body and mind in the present.

Feeling more comfortable? Your ready to experience something new about relaxation…

Relaxation

---

*"Our bodies are our gardens, our
wills are gardeners."*

- William Shakespeare

Some think of relaxation as sitting in front of the TV, going
to the pub, spending time with family or friends. These may
be relaxing times, but they still require a degree of emotional,
mental and physical stimulation. True relaxation is a moment
of emotional, mental and physical quiet. Your breathing and
heart-rate slows, your muscles relax and you feel calm and at
peace in your body.

Close your eyes if you want.

Take a deep breath and clench a fist tightly and hold for three
seconds, imagining the tension in the fist as a colour, light
or electricity, something which will represent the tension for
you.

Relax your fist as you exhale slowly. Imagine the muscle tension change colour, light blue or green can work well, or change
the substance, feel it dissolving or melting away. Notice the

difference in your hand before and after it was clenched and the relaxation you should feel now.

Do the same with your other hand and in the future, you can clench both hands at the same time.

Breath in slowly, carry on with the muscles of both arms, really tense them, imagine the colours or shapes, however you imagine the tension to be, then release and exhale as the colour or shape changes. Let the arms relax and enjoy the feeling.

What other part of your body do you think we'll relax next?

Onto your face. Really scrunch your face up and notice how good it feels when you relax it.

Shrug your shoulders, hold, then go through the relaxation procedure. Just let go.

Next your chest and back, start to feel like a rag doll.

Now onto your waist.

Proceed to your hips and buttocks, tense and relax them.

As you breath out, you might think about the feelings in your legs. Tense your thighs, let them go. Feel yourself sinking into the floor.

The calf muscles getting loose and limp, sinking down.

Finally your feet, all tension draining away.

Isn't it interesting how your body relaxes without trying too hard. Enjoy the feeling of calm. You can go through this exercise as many times as you wish, just notice how relaxed you feel at the end.

You are able to do it quickly. Tense and relax the upper body as a whole, then the lower body, then the legs. Fielders need to relax between balls to keep themselves fresh mentally. Fielding on the boundary, you get a detached view where you could notice a flaw in the batsman's game. Wicket keepers can use physical relaxation to stay alert while the bowler is walking away before turning to start his run.

You can utilise this relaxed state by making positive suggestions to yourself.

Another way to do this is without tensing the muscles, perhaps just before sleep as you lie in bed as physically tensing your muscles may keep you awake. Imagine a wave of relaxation soothing it's way down through your body, maybe it's a soft colour, one that can really relax you, going into every fibre of your body. Remember a time and place of peace, a sanctuary perhaps or gazing at the stars on a clear summer evening or lying on the beach, hearing the waves gently lap on the sea shore. Engage in the moment.

How about active relaxation. I'll illustrate this with a story. Several members of a team were told to sprint 800 metres as fast as they could, the time was recorded. Next, the coach instructed them to sprint the same distance, only this time at just 90% of effort. Their time was better the second time. Why? Your muscles are organised into opposing pairs. Running along with many other activities are performed most effectively when some muscles are contracting, while others are relaxing. While sprinting at top speed. You use all of your leg muscles so they are actually working against themselves, accelerating and breaking at the same time. This prevents you running as fast as you can. As a paradox, running at 90% effort, you are relaxing the muscles enough to stop them hindering maximum effort.

The same can be said about bowling. Trying to bowl as hard as you can uses all the muscles in the arm-so working against themselves. It's a bit like 'Ready, Fire, Aim!' To achieve accuracy and speed, the biceps need to relax, while the triceps do the work so you get 'Ready, Aim, Fire!'

Here's an ideal way to produce instant, physical relaxation which comes from Yoga. Breath through your eyes. That's right. Imagine as you inhale, the air your breathing is entering your body through your eyes. You can actually feel your muscles relax if your eyes are open, or shut. It happens all by itself!

Now you know how to relax and use your imagination, lets see how you ask questions…

Creative Questions

" If you fail to plan, plan to fail. "

- John Wooden

Asking questions is about the easiest and one of the most powerful tools you can use to transform yourself for the better and challenge your mind.

Questions direct your focus of attention. If your spin bowling is poor, notice how you question your spin bowling ability. Simply ask yourself 'How can I ask this in a positive way?' which makes your questions more empowering.

Many sportspeople get frustrated because they ask themselves negative questions. 'Why can't I…?' To understand the question, your mind automatically looks for the reason why you can't. But no matter what the answer is, you are still accepting the fact that you can't do it. Your also reinforcing the problem in your mind. Here's a trick. Change 'why' into 'how'. Ask yourself 'how can I do this'. This assumes it can be done and there can be a number of ways it can be done, so the question allows your mind to search out a positive solution.

You'll be surprised to discover how you can go further. You might ask 'how should I train in the nets today?' Instead ask 'how should I train in the nets today to enjoy every minute?'

So, ask questions that focus on the positive:
How can this stamina problem be solved easily?
How many different ways can I guard against batting faults?
How can I stop inconsistent run-up?
How am I going to become…?

These questions put your brain into a more resourceful state. If your not happy with an answer, change the way you ask the question. Your brain will keep searching until a happy solution is found. It's good to know that your unconscious has the answer to all the questions you'll ever ask. You can allow new answers to come to you.

Ask yourself these:

Do you love the game so much you'd pay to play it?
How passionate do you feel about cricket? Bowling, batting, fielding?
What would you do if you had unlimited ability?

Curiosity creates questions. By bringing your vivid imagination into play as you ask creative questions, you build up a vivid representation of the answer, then amplify it, make it a sensory-rich experience, turn the colours brighter, the sounds louder, the feelings stronger. By regularly concentrating on what you want, you condition your mind to attract more of it.

If you ever find it hard to bring an answer to mind, remember the solution to it! Remembrance was an old philosophers trick. Instead of asking your mind to search for an answer to a challenge, simply ask your mind to remember it. Again the presupposition that you once knew the answer creates a mindset that the answer actually exists, so eliminates the anxiety of helplessness you may endure.

Many apprehensions and worries are often caused by not giving your mind something better to do. Look at it this way, the one asking the question is usually the one holding the cards.

Good answers from good questions often come to you through rest...

Rest

"The ancestor of every action is a thought."

- Ralph Waldo Emerson

Both your mind and body have their own way to rest and recharge their batteries. This happens about every 90 minutes when they stop external focus and spend around 15 minutes to rest and replenish. This is known as the ultradian rhythm when you find yourself daydreaming and a soft feeling of comfort begins in your body. People constantly ignore these signs so go into overload. If you go with it, you will feel refreshed and have better concentration after.

Deepen the experience by self-hypnosis, meditation, or listen to relaxing music. Imagine yourself in a favourite place, an exotic beach, an oasis of peace and calm, a garden, somewhere that is special for you. Your nervous system can't tell the difference between a real or an imagined event, so fool it into believing it's on holiday.

Try this exercise to improve well-being once or twice a day, it doesn't take long and is a variation on the relaxation exercise I described earlier.

Put your attention on your feet and notice any feeling in them, coldness, warmth, weight.

Take a deep breath and as you exhale, imagine a warm, pleasant feeling begin in your feet. You can imagine a colour.

When your ready take another deep breath and imagine that warm, relaxed feeling travelling up to your knees. As it does, say a word like 'relax', 'rest', 'peace', or give each stage a number. Let that comfortable feeling penetrate your muscles and bones, soothing them.

When your ready, take another gentle breath and imagine the feeling rising up to your waist and repeat your special word or the next number.

With the same breathing pattern, let that feeling of ease and relaxation arrive at your shoulders, soothing them as you say your special word.

Next let that relaxation flow from your shoulders down your arms and into your hands and fingers.

Again breath and let the feeling flow all the way up your face to the top of your head. Say the word or number and let the feeling spread all over your body.

In your mind say the word and imagine the relaxation double and float down from your head so it mixes with those good feelings already going on inside your body.

As this relaxation drifts down your body, imagine any tension being washed down and away out of your feet so it makes room for new, refreshing energy spreading down from your head, until you feel your body glow with energy from your head to your feet.

Now take a few moments to really bask in that feeling of re-laxation.

If you want, do it again. The more you practice the better it becomes.

Just allow whatever happens to happen and feel satisfied with what your accomplishing.

Maybe you will think about goals...

Goals

"People are not lazy. They simply have impotent goals-that is, goals that do not inspire them. "

- Anthony Robbins

Can't get enough now, can you? A goal is a mental representation of something you wish to achieve within a given time frame. Aiming for goals is a simple way to keep yourself motivated, evaluate progress, create emotion and achieve things. A goal can give you clearer direction. If you don't know where your going, you'll probably end up somewhere else.

What would you do if you knew you couldn't fail? Goals can stop you stumbling through life. Why leave things to chance. Goals can help you move away from your limitations. Goals can make you the teams No1 pace bowler.

Focus your mind on a target and your more likely to achieve it. If you don't aim for goals, your efforts (arrows) will go astray. Set time limits, but keep them flexible, reaching the goal is the important element, not the time frame. If you can't reach the time frame, just reassess the goal and keep on until it is reached. And focus on what you want rather than what you don't want.

A well known acronym for setting goals is SMART. The S is for Specific. Be careful about specific. 'I want to score fifty runs a game' is specific. What happens when you've scored your fifty? 'OUT' can be heard. 'I want to score more than fifty runs a game' gets you a good innings and gives you room to go further. M is Measurable. Create a starting-point from where you can measure your improvements. A stands for Achievable. High enough to inspire solid hope of reaching it. R is Realistic. If the target is too far away, it can damage your motivation. And T is Time-bound, an accomplishment date. Make it challenging. A goal is a dream with a target.

What do you want to accomplish in Cricket? It starts when you set goals. It's the first step into putting your dreams into action.

Ask goal oriented questions:
What do you want from cricket? Is it specific, definite, measurable?
Can you maintain your goal?
What stops you having that goal?
What resources have you? Are they emotional, financial, mental, physical, spiritual?
What resources are required?

On a scale of 1-10, what would 10 be like as your very best? What would 1 be like? What's the closest to 10 you've been? Where are you on that scale now? What would it take to go 2 points higher? I bet you can do twice as good as your doing.

How you design your goals makes a big difference. The bigger the better. Your goal should excite and scare you at the same time. If it frightens you, you are facing your fear of failure, but your not backing down. Break the ultimate goal down into smaller parts until each step is easy for you to take action. By having a number of smaller chunks to work on stops you freaking out over a large overwhelming one. State goals with joy and act as if they were already a reality. Read or recite your goal every day. Your mind needs constant repetitions to accept your aims deeply and unconsciously. Be consistent.

When you set your sights on a goal whole-heartedly, your unconscious will do what it can to help you reach it. It doesn't take much to get things started, a simple thought or action. Or even better, a thought and action combined.

Here's one goal you should aim for. Learn the Laws of Cricket, particularly the LBW and No Ball rules. It's important that you totally understand these as they have an influence on your performance.

Goals give you growth. They can transform your life. Grab any evidence that shows you are achieving your target or that motivates you. Hold it in your hands, smell it, let it shine on you. Expect that standing ovation.

I cover more on goals in the Self-Hypnosis for Cricket manual which comes later.

Lets change any negative self-talk by reframing…

Reframing

"Little things affect little minds."

- Benjamin Disraeli

Failure is not the end result. Some people see failure as an excuse to give up, others think about failure so much, it becomes the best way to repeat it. Others, you included, can see things in a positive light by reframing any situation. The glass becomes half-full, never half-empty. You are in control. Reframing gives you the flexibility to make situations work for you.

In training, do you think you may never reach the required level? Do you worry you'll lose the next game? Thoughts like these hamper performance. If your afraid of losing, your dominant thought is about losing. Winners think about the next game and how to win it, losers think about the last one and who to blame. Notice your thoughts and change them to positives.

When you come across an opponent who is bigger, fitter, faster, more experienced than you, don't tell yourself s/he is better than you. Use your internal dialogue to put the person down, ridicule them. Play on any weakness, real or perceived.

Change their appearance, remember how to do that in the imagination chapter? This gives your mind something to do and gives you the confidence to face them. More relaxed, you can focus more easily on your strategy and stop any self-talk of fear or tension.

Positive thinking helps you realise there are limitations in any opponents ability as explained in the Imagination chapter. If your opponent is larger than you, tell yourself 'being bigger s/he will be to slow or clumsy, there's no way s/he is going to keep up with me, I'm more agile, slimmer, faster.'

If your opponent is smaller, maybe faster than you, its probable s/he will be physically weaker. 'I'm stronger, I'll hit the ball all over the field'. Look for their weaknesses, not strengths and create emotion when you speak to yourself, be elated, believe you have the skill to defeat your opponent.

Know that if you play with performance damaging thoughts, you are able to change or remove them. To make any negative emotion disappear, amend the thought. Change any colour, put a frame around it, make it smaller, further away, make it darker. Move the sound, change it. When you have changed the negative emotion, repeat several times so it can't affect you again.

Another reframe can be done if you don't usually get pictures or sounds, but experience negative feelings. This is similar to moving the voice in The Inner Critic chapter:

Where is the feeling? Move it to your thumb, or big toe.
Does it have a shape? Change the shape.
What texture does it have? Change that.
What temperature has it? Make it cold or warm.
Change any element until all the negative feeling is eliminated.

Whenever you realise you have made a negative statement, restate what you said into a positive

one by beginning the sentence with 'in the past.' So, 'I'm always lbw against left-armers' can now become 'In the past I used to be lbw by left-armers.'

Reframing can transform you, bring hope from hopelessness, turn despair into delight, build success from apathy. As with everything taught here, you have to practice, then practice some more, but once you know it, you have it for life.

New thinking = Better thinking = Better ability = Better You.

Change your thinking, change your Cricket. Go for the change, don't be afraid.

Reframing can be helped by anchoring...

Anchoring

> **❝** *Don't find fault, find a remedy.* **❞**
>
> - Henry Ford

Remember how you can use The Circle of Excellence to bring about a resourceful state, so with Anchoring. It's like having a 'push button' to feel excellence.

Have you come across an old photo which created a pang of emotion? Heard an old song which was popular during a special time of your life? Smelt a particular aroma that brought memories rushing back? Do you frequently visit a location and always sit at the same place?

All these associations trigger memories that take us back to a past experience. They are called Anchors as they 'anchor' you to a certain state. The clever thing is you can use these 'anchors' to bring back the whole experience.

Create a physical signal which you are going to use. What you read in many NLP books is touch your thumb and forefinger together, but it can be anything you think is appropriate, patting down you hair, scratching an imaginary itch, clasping your hands, rubbing a wrist, crossing fingers. It's up to you.

Now, think of a time when you had the ability or emotion you want to repeat. Add as much detail as you can, remember, see what you saw, hear what you heard, feel how you felt then. Now see, hear, feel all even more fully, experience it intensely. Let it all come back to you, let it build up so you relive it in your whole body. If you can't remember a time, imagine how you would feel if you had the confidence or success.

As the memory 'peaks' fire the physical signal, sink into the feeling of being there. Again make it brighter, richer, turn up the volume.

Now break state by doing something like remembering a friends telephone number, saying your name backwards, or reciting a nursery rhyme so when you repeat this technique, it's like doing it afresh.

Now repeat four or five times. You can bring in different, positive memories if you wish, rather than doing the same one.

Test to see if the anchor works. Break state by thinking of something else. Then fire your anchor. You should get back into the resourceful state.

The great thing with using anchors is they work automatically. Think about a forthcoming event when you will require that feeling or emotion. Imagine everything going perfectly. Picture it in your mind, seeing, hearing, feeling yourself in this good state at that future time. Now fire your anchor.

You see how you can become 'anchored' to certain states, you may even have created un-resourceful states for yourself in the past. We all have negative anchors which can be disconnected by a process called 'collapsing anchors'.

Fully remember an unwanted state or memory, for example lets say 'apprehensive.' Re-live it and when you feel the emotion, anchor it kinaesthetically somewhere on your body, say for example your left knee.

Break state by thinking of something else. This is important.

Now, access fully a positive state or memory you have experienced, lets go for 'competent' and anchor that kinaesthetically somewhere else, this time the right knee.

Break state.

Now fire both anchors simultaneously. As long as the resourceful states anchor is stronger than the undesired states, the undesired anchor will collapse and the un-resourceful state will no longer affect you. If you picked a strong negative memory, you may need more resources to make the situation more satisfying.

Practice anchoring to place yourself into more resourceful states. Do it when your in different positions or environments. Go to different locations and practice getting yourself into positive moods. You can look back with satisfaction to see how much further you have developed.

Next is a method to overcome internal conflict…

Internal Conflict

> *"Failure is an attitude, not an outcome."*
>
> - Harvey Mackay

You're the batsman standing alone at the wicket. Part of you may have the confidence to take on everything, while another part of you may want to be cautious, as it will keep the wicket safe. A tug-of-war between ambition versus performance anxiety. Two conflicting beliefs you have for the same situation will only hold you back. If you are indecisive in your mind, how is your body going to know what to do?

If two incompatible states occur at the same time, you can modify each and reform them into a third state, which is an integration of the original two.

Throughout this manual, you will learn methods which will get your mind working. Some may seem silly, others uncomfortable. Some may challenge your way of thinking, change does that. Take it as a good sign-it's not for the faint-hearted.

This process can cause changes.

Taking the example of two conflicting beliefs above, find a quiet place where your not going to be disturbed and get yourself relaxed. Think about the situation causing internal conflict.

Place your hands in front of yourself, palms up. Imagine the confident part in your dominant hand. See it as a colour, shape, a person, anything to make it real for you.

Do the same with your other hand, where you place your cautious part.

Ask the confident hand what it's positive intention is for you. Continue asking until you get the feeling of an answer, even if you think your imagining it.

Now ask the cautious hand what it's positive intention is for you.

Keep asking until you recognise on some level, they both want the same outcome. Go through the process even if you think your imagination is playing tricks, it's not.

This is for reference:

Confident Part = more courage = perform better = success.
Cautious Part = anxious = safety = success.

Now imagine a Successful Part is there between your hands possessing the resources of confidence and caution.

Slowly bring your hands together until those two separate Parts become an integrated whole.

Bring your joined hands up to your chest and imagine your allowing the new integrated Part to step inside you. Convinced?

Next is a slightly different and quicker method to change a negative response into a positive.

Bring to mind a problem or bad memory you have. What would it's solution or opposite be where you want a desirable outcome?

Place your non-dominant hand about 18 inches in front of your face and project your problem onto it. Have your dominant hand behind your back.

Practice by changing hands so your dominant hand is before your face, the other behind your back. Now project the solution onto your dominant hand.

Now you know the movement, get set up as before with the 'problem hand' before your face and as fast as you can, change hands. You can even use a motivational word as you change.

Break state by shaking your hands off, repeating your telephone number, or use some other distraction.

Repeat ten times. You should neutralise the problem and replace it with a beneficial condition.

As you practice this it gets easier to resolve any internal conflict. You can hold onto your seat as your entering the world where there are no limitations.

Lets talk about motivation...

Motivation

"You just can't beat a person who never gives up."

- Babe Ruth

Motivation is a much used word in sport. It comes from the Latin word meaning 'to move.' The most important thing for you however is to love your Cricket.

Most people can access unhappiness, guilt, even depression quite easily. By thinking of some failure in your life you open up undesirable emotions. The opposite can be the same. You can feel confident, excited, happy , you don't have to have a reason!

When you have played well, you can repeat it by accessing the same levels of arousal that you experienced at that good time.

Here are some methods to increase motivation:

Change livens things up, can you vary your training routine, different exercise, new place?

Decreasing your rate of breathing will affect your nervous system. Slow, deep breathing through your nose creates relaxation in body and mind.

Someone could call nervous energy before a game anxiety, you could label it excitement. Rename nervousness, boredom, drudgery to something more inspiring. How does 'another type of excitement' sound, or 'adventurous'.

Release any tense, nervous energy by moving the muscles before any game. Tense and relax each muscle group. You should do this during a warm up anyway. A fielder can shift from foot to foot to sway into a calm, relaxed state of awareness.

Use key words that can excite, or inspire you. 'Easy', 'power', 'winner', even your name or team name. Create words or phrases that are personal, but powerful for you.

Use upbeat music to arouse you. On the pitch, play it in your head.

Suppose you have a boring task ahead of you. Picture something that motivates you, then trick yourself into changing the chore so it looks and feels exactly the same as the one that gets you going. As you've learnt, altering the variables, brightness, colour, position, shape, size, sound, can change how you react.

These are the steps:

Remember something that pleased you, a triumph you would wish to experience again. Maybe the result of your last over. Concentrate on that image while you ask yourself:

Is it a still picture or a movie?
Is it in colour or black and white?
Is it close to you or further away?

What size?

Are you inside it, like it's wrapped around you, or outside and your looking in?

If any movement, is it fast or slow?

If the image is in front of you, are you looking from above, or below it?

Look at the boring task you want to feel motivated about. Ask yourself the same questions and notice what's different or the same about the two pictures?

Move the unmotivated picture into the space occupied by the triumphant picture. Change everything to make it look and feel the same as the triumphant picture.

Intensify it, make it vibrant. Give it more of what you've given it. Hear the band playing a theme tune. Even imagine pressure on your back as if someone was pushing you into the picture. Make it real.

Do this change quickly, forcefully. Do it five times, breaking the state between each change, so your starting as new, each time.

By telling your brain to represent the tedious picture in this exciting new way, the happy changes you make tell your brain 'I don't want this…I want this'. So, how do you feel about the boring task? It should feel better, more achievable.

Remember earlier, by changing 'why' into 'how' can be inspiring? Here's another word to change to get that motivation flowing. 'Should' gives people a feeling of guilt when they 'should do…' but don't. Turn it into 'want'. 'I should practice leg spin,' 'I should concentrate when fielding,' how do they make you feel in your body? Let it become 'I want to practice leg spin,' I want to concentrate when fielding,'. Is that 'want' feeling different from the 'should'? Has it made you more determined? Does it give you a prideful desire to achieve? 'want power' can be as good as 'will power.'

As I have mentioned, use language carefully. Words represent something, they're like symbols. Your words literary can become your world. Here are some more you can play with. Turn 'but' into 'and,' 'if' into 'when,' 'why' can also become 'because.' Here's some more, 'hopefully' or 'might' can be 'I'm going to' or 'I am capable.' These words and phrases can be more motivating.

Complete these positive statements:

I am in the process of…
I've decided…
It excites me when…

Lets investigate the power of Mirroring…

Mirroring

> **"***A champion is afraid of losing, everyone
> else is afraid of winning.* **"**
>
> - Billie Jean King

Anything practiced continuously over time becomes an automatic behaviour. Problems arise when the practice is not perfect. If it's not spot-on, the cricketer creates a varied pathway to the required standard, resulting in poor performance.

If your new to cricket, or about to take on an unfamiliar role, wicket keeper for example, you have nothing to personally use as a reference to achieving a particular level. Copy the same things in the same way as someone who has excelled at it. Do the same things in the same way as someone who has done it successfully.

Choose a skill you would like to master. Imagine what having that ability can do for you. If you can, remember in the past having done the skill to the level you want.

Choose a role model, someone you respect and admire, who easily exhibits that skill. Someone who has walked that road.

Become a director and make a movie in your mind of your hero demonstrating that skill effortlessly. Press play and watch carefully your hero doing everything perfectly from beginning to end. Watch out for any distinctions you need to note.

Observe how your role model carries her/himself? How do they move? Imagine how they talk to themselves positively.

This time play the movie again, including yourself beside or behind your role model, imitating their actions, breathing, voice, mimic everything exactly.

Now climb in and disguise yourself as your hero, synchronise fully. Modify everything until the animation is exactly as you wish. See through their eyes, hear through their ears, take on the feelings of how empowered s/he is.

Feel what it's like to be your role model having that skill. Build up the feelings, sounds, sights. See all around you how other people respond.

How different does your future look. How much more optimism do you have as a result of this perfect skill? Live this future, make it real for yourself.

Step out and away and imagine in front of you the other you who now exhibits the skills, assurance, energy you have made your own. Make any modifications.

If your role model has written instructions in a book or manual, or had themselves filmed, get a copy to study. Do research. Find out what the person did to find success. Understand how they think.

Continue to rehearse until you are certain you can perform their skill automatically. Even if you feel like your making it up, your teaching your brain a new behaviour, so pretend until it becomes natural.

Maybe imagine once or twice not doing as well so you can bring your emotions into it. Don't just visualize the best-case scenarios. Be prepared with a plan B and also a plan C. Don't imagine failing, but mentally plan how you will respond to unpleasant or difficult situations. This happens sooner or later when games don't go exactly as you hoped. You can still be proud of putting 100% effort in.

Pretend you're an exceptional cricketer, act as if it were true and soon your mind will forget to pretend, you've mastered it.

Feeling good? Want to create happiness on demand?

You can with the inner smile...

The Inner Smile

" There's more ways of getting out than is shown in t'rules. "

- Wilfred Rhodes

When your happy your body creates a chemical, serotonin, or the 'happy chemical'. It releases tension, control's pain, gives your immune system a boost and promotes well-being throughout your body.

Remember times when you were happy and light-hearted. If you can't think of a particular time, how about a comedy show or film, even jokes you've heard. Go over them while you turn up the brightness, the colour, the sounds, make them richer, remember how good you felt until you find yourself smiling with pure joy. Double that feeling. Do it again. How do you feel?

Imagine now how better your life can be if you were like this all the time.

Vividly imagine your eyes smiling, a glint in them dancing there. Raise the corners of your mouth as if you have a special secret. You use more facial muscles when you smile than when you frown, so give them a good workout.

Get a sense of where that feeling is the strongest. Play with it some more. Increase it, give it a happy colour and roll it up to the top of your head and down to the bottom of your feet. Imagine every cell glowing with delight.

You can do this anywhere. It's good to imagine all the benefits this is going to give you, isn't it?

Put a smile anywhere in your body that feels uncomfortable or tense. When you think about relationships, training, games, smile with the same energy and notice your mood begin to lift.

Here's a bonus. These happy chemicals create more connections in the brain every time you have a pleasant experience. So not only can your body experience happiness, the more often it happens, the more intelligent you become. What was a technique has now become a positive attitude. And the more positive you can be with relationships…

Relationships

"It's a funny kind of month, October. For the really keen cricket fan it's when you realise your wife left you in May."

- Denis Norden

This chapter is on the basis of people you know involved in cricket.

Often it's not the opposition that can be a barrier, but family, friends, work colleagues or team mates who are the problem. 'You'll never be good enough' or 'don't set your sights too high'. As well-meaning as they think they are, it's easier to make a player worse than better. Have you ever noticed how expert some people can be about things they don't really have a clue about? If you take notice of people who tell you what you can't do, you will never accomplish anything. Your placed in a negative frame of mind, have a conflict of priorities and it all spills over into a poor sporting performance.

You get intolerant coach's who think they're being helpful by criticising you. Some players respond well to that, but not all. 'You'll never be a batsman' doesn't work for everyone. Often you go onto the pitch and make mistakes because a negative expectation has been set up in your mind.

Almost everyday, the sport pages print embarrassing and sometimes tragic stories of car crashes, drunken behaviour, drug suspensions, gambling. Lives and careers have been ruined by the poor choices sports people have made.

Have you had an argument with someone, maybe the captain and hours later your still re-living it, still seeing the captains face and hearing the words. If you change the picture and sounds as described in the chapter on Imagination, you can change your feelings.

What about a conflict of ideas with a coach, official or team mate? Perhaps you should consider what they have said before dismissing it. The truth can hurt sometimes, but putting yourself in others shoes, makes you adaptable so can give you further insight:

Go to a time when you had a difference of opinion with someone. Visualise that person stood before you now, notice all the detail.

Now step out of your body and let any emotions go. This will soon start to make sense.

Step into their body and notice the world from their perspective, seeing, hearing, feeling and thinking from their point of view.

Next, step away from their body and let their feelings go.

Think of someone you admire. A friend, hero, even a character from the past who is mature, intelligent and wise. Step into their body and see that person considering you and your foe from a neutral position.

Are there any insights you can find. What advice would this mentor give you?

Lastly, step back into your own body taking with you anything you have learned. Can you move toward a resolution? Do you see things different?

A key to reaching your potential is learn to listen to others. Lean toward them when they speak. Place your tongue on the roof of your mouth, this quietens internal dialogue so you can pay attention to the other person. Don't interrupt or finish other's sentences. People will appreciate your listening skills. If someone interrupts while your speaking, politely ask them to wait until you have finished then you will listen while they speak.

Most Cricketers don't get to play in a Test Match. Follow your goals and not the crowd. You may feel envious when your friends go to parties, often the parties aren't that much anyway. You can make up for it later. Avoid people and distractions that can turn you away from your dreams. Sometimes you may have to let go of old friendships if a fire to succeed in Cricket burns in you.

One of the best ways to improve is mix with successful, skilful people. Surround yourself with achievers who provide good teaching and will make you better. Find a few people, Cricketers, umpires, sport journalists, anyone who understand the game. Invite them out for a drink or a meal. Be cheeky, write to them for advice. Let them know you want to pick their brains on how you can be a success. They become aware of you and understand you are serious. Be humble. Listen. As long as your respectful, most people will enjoy the opportunity to help you. Other people can also see situations without the emotional baggage you may carry.

Ask those involved in the game to tell you what they would tell another player how to beat you. What are your strong points and weak ones. How they see your vulnerable.

Praise others also. Being critical, judgemental or opinionated are three ways to see relationships disappear. Use integrity. Impart sound knowledge and experience to junior players, set an example.

Excitement and passion are contagious. Don't allow others to put you off, or pull you down. And remember, scientists proved bumblebees couldn't fly. But the scientists didn't tell the bumblebees. You have more potential than you, or others realise.

Next lets look at the interesting subject of time management...

Time Management

" Put your hand on a hot stove for a minute,
it seems like an hour. Sit with a pretty girl for
an hour, it seems like a minute. "

- Albert Einstein

Most of us find it difficult to live in the present, we think about past experiences and worry about future ones. Time passes at different rates for each of us. Your unconscious mind doesn't compare time passing by the same as your conscious mind, which does so by a clock, watch or other time piece.

Time varies depending on the circumstances you find yourself in. When your nervous, in pain, or sad, time slows down. The clock seems to drag, a couple of minutes are like half-an-hour, or even stands still.

Long boring periods waiting to go out to bat can cause the batsman to lose concentration and sharpness. For any position, Test cricket can be a long game.

In contrast, when your excited and happy, maybe having a great game, the time flashes by.

You can manipulate time if you imagine a situation and slow the process right down to practice and improve a skill. I'll show you. Lets take bowling.

Get yourself into a relaxed state. If your better closing your eyes, do so. Hold a real ball in your hand. If you can't, pretend you have one. Feel it's weight, the coolness. Notice the stitching at the seam, the smell of it.

Carefully examine the correct movements of bowling. Feel for yourself the whole process of delivery, go through each step so you can physically remember the movements of grip, arm, shoulder, don't forget the run up involving hips, legs, feet.

See each element in slow motion, at a snails pace. Go over them several times making sure the feel of each element is right. When your happy, speed it all up. Imagine yourself bowl as you would for real. Feel mighty, make everything colourful, vivid, see the batsman, despondent as you intimidate him. See him successfully bowled out, the ball smashing through the stumps.

What if your batting? Do the same only this time feel the bat in your hands. Smell the oiled willow, bring in every sense while you stand comfortable, feeling more and more relaxed, you have plenty of time. Again start in slow motion so your technique is correct, then speed up for real time. You are more prepared to face a fast bowler and score runs by avoiding risk. As you focus on the frustrated bowler, see the hundred-mile-per-hour ball coming toward you at a slow rate. Hear the sweet spot connect as you send the ball flying.

With every mental rehearsal, detail will increase. The practice you can make in your mind in a few minutes, would require hours of practice in real time. Your unconscious can't tell the difference between what's real and what's imagined, which is why this technique is perfect if your out through injury. It can help keep you focused.

Enjoy the activity as you see yourself perform at your best. And give yourself positive suggestions.

Here's an easy activity to help you place cricket as your number one daily priority. Get yourself a calendar, diary or inexpensive day planner. If it pictures cricket so much the better. Start your day with it by writing down the time you plan to train, play competitively or read a motivational book or magazine, then plan the rest of your day around that event, no matter what. Make this commitment holy. You have made cricket your top priority and arrange everything else around it rather than 'trying to fit cricket in'.

In the next chapter your going to learn to conquer fear...

Fear (False Evidence Appearing Real)

> *"It's not a question of getting rid of but-*
> *terflies, it's a question of getting them to fly in*
> *formation."*
>
> - John Donohue

We all have a primitive fight or flight response built into us for survival. This response will be explained more fully in the Pain Control chapter. We either fight, or flee from whatever is threatening us. Today, most of our dangers aren't a threat to life and limb, but a psychological threat to our self-esteem and ego.

What I'm going to discuss here is not a sporting technique itself, however some players go through anxieties during their Cricket careers. Your uneasy in lifts, your afraid of cats, dogs, birds. You don't like flying and your team is off to a foreign location. Worry about your most intimidating opponent who you soon have to face makes your stomach tremble. As you can see, fear creates limitations for you and can turn into a phobia.

You weren't born with a fear or a phobia. Many phobias can be traced back to an unpleasant incident when you were younger. Your elder brother may have locked you in a cupboard when you were a young child. What if the dark cupboard was full of moths, or even spiders! Since then, whenever you see moths or spiders or you are in an enclosed space, you relive the event.

The fear of failure prevents people from reaching their full potential. That fear of failure prevents most Cricketers from succeeding than any opponent. Fear actually creates the situations that stop Cricketers from winning. A paradox of sport is that fear of failure actually makes failure more likely. You bat defensively when intuition tells you to go on the offence. You're afraid of losing, of making mistakes, but just as afraid of winning. The thought of the consequences inhibits you. Fear makes you play safe. Fear makes you play small.

An injury can create a fear response as you may be scared of hurting yourself again, then suffering through the agony of more recovery time. A fielder may hesitate about diving for a passing ball after he damaged his collar bone a previous time.

Look at it this way, a fear, even a phobia, is an overcompensating protection mechanism. You didn't learn it, you overlearned it and the good news is because it was learned, it can be unlearned.

Your unconscious raises it's head when you feel overwhelmed in any way. Warning you to be cautious, anxious, fearful. Now some lucky people can use these feelings as excitement. But you may be nervous about the bounce, length, deviation or pace of a delivery as you go out to bat and that feeling starts. Acknowledge your unconscious, thank it for the warning, it's done it's job, now let it go. You don't need its presence, now switch your focus to getting on with the job at hand and take care of what you need to concentrate on.

This following technique is known in NLP as the 'Fast Phobia Cure' or the 'Movie Theatre' technique:

Close your eyes and get yourself comfortable. Give this your full involvement. Imagine your sat in a cinema, you can remember a real one if you wish. The screen is blank. Your in charge of the remote control there in your hand.

On a scale of 1-10, 1 hardly being anything, 10 being severe, what number is the problem your having?

In a moment your going to play a movie of yourself and the problem you have. As it's a past event, the movie has aged, so it's poor quality and the colour has faded, even turned sepia. You will play your movie in a rectangle in the centre of the screen, not all of the screen.

Compose a comical theme tune, something like The Muppets, Monty Python, Popeye or similar.

Before you press play, remember a time when you know you were confident, excited, or successful. Feel all that good energy and let it spread all around your body, now intensify it. Turn up the volume. Maintain that good feeling while you watch the movie. You may even use Anchoring to create a resourceful state if the fear your facing should get out of hand.

Now pay attention. Behind you is the projection booth. To get further distance from your fear, imagine yourself leaving your body sat there in the chair and floating up back toward the projection booth. From here, you can observe yourself watching the movie, watching yourself.

You will play the film of your bad event from beginning to end where it will then freeze-frame. Go ahead and press play on the remote.

When the film reaches that last frame press stop. Now watch yourself in the cinema seat rise and go up there to the still picture and congratulate the younger you for being so brave for going through and surviving that nasty experience. It's as if you see yourself from the fan's perspective, or your coaches. Your safe. With that acknowledgement watch yourself return to your seat.

When your ready, run the whole film backwards at top speed, hearing that comical music play. Then play the movie forwards then backwards at fast speed several times. How do you feel? Is there a difference to the memory? On a scale of 1-10, where is it now? Has the old response gone? If so float back down to your seat and feeling fully whole again, rise and exit the cinema.

We all get anxious but people plagued by fear get anxious about being anxious. Accept fear and recognise it as the body's way of telling you to become energised. You can then face any difficulty and come out smiling.

Or try Spinning…

Spinning

"Life's too short to be afraid."

- Robbie Williams

This is a simple, quick-fix technique taught by Paul McKenna, who I acknowledge here for it. You may find it interesting. It's ideal when you find yourself in a shaky or stressful situation which needs to be addressed there and then. The concept is all feelings start in one place within your body and move in a prescribed direction and so by reversing the direction of the bad feeling, you can eliminate it.

Go through this routine while thinking about your problem. Say poor ability to judge the length from a very fast bowler. On a scale of 1-10, 1 being almost nothing and 10 being extremely uncomfortable, where are you at the moment?

Think about what's disturbing you and get an idea of where that feeling begins. Usually it's around the stomach/solar plexus and moves upward toward your throat.

Imagine lifting that feeling out of your body and watching it spin before you like a wheel.

Imagine what colour it is. Now change that colour to your favourite.

Maybe imagine a pleasant noise or music.

With a flip, turn the wheel upside down so that it spins in the opposite direction.

When you feel calmer about the situation, pull the wheel back into your body to where it started, still spinning in the opposite direction

Let it speed up, faster and faster, until the anxiety or upset begins to fade away and finally disappear. On the scale of 1-10, where do you find the problem now? You may now be able to build up your innings. Problems can vanish entirely.

You can also replace an undesirable state with a desirable one using Swish…

Swish

"I can change! You can change! Everybody can certainly change!"

\- Rocky IV

This strategy can bring freedom to self-doubt. The trick is to have your positive image on the catapult in it's high-tension position ready to fire so that your mind accepts the image as going one way-toward you.

First in front of you place a picture of an image you would like of yourself, assertive, powerful, something that can give you goose bumps of excitement, or remember a memory you would like to change. Something that is realistic and attainable. Make it exciting. Have it full of the skills or qualities you would like more of, a natural catcher, a stroke master. Make the details vivid, see yourself oozing with confidence then make it larger, the colours bright, add sparkle, play a theme tune that's up-beat, adding vitality. Add approving voices of coaches or team mates. Make everything rich and intense. I really want you to live in this so include anything that improves the image.

Imagine this picture of your image has thick rubber bands attached to each corner and are fixed to a firing mechanism somewhere behind you. The picture is slowly pulled away from you, stretching off into the distance on those rubber bands, so that it seems like a giant catapult is being aimed at you ready to fire. Lock that exciting picture in place and be aware of the tension in those stretched rubber bands. Your hands are on the firing lever.

Bring up a second image or a memory before you of whatever it is that's giving you a lack of confidence, fear, inertia, under-performance, where you would benefit from a new self-image. Lets say slow hands behind the wicket. Drain away any colour, turn down the focus, shrink it down, quieten any sound.

Before you fire the first, good image, think of a motivational word. Originally it used to be 'Swish' as that is how therapists had the two images interchanged, but any word appropriate to you or the situation can be more effective.

When your ready, feel yourself fire the catapult so that the exciting image shoots up right in front of you, its acceleration tearing through that poor second image or memory, so you end with that exciting first picture before you. If it's done fast enough, you may even jump. Don't forget to add the inspiring word.

Notice any changes to how you feel. Reset the positive image by stretching back the elastic band again under tension so you have before you the remnants of a broken second image of what had made you feel bad. With that poor picture in front of you, fire again so that the good one once again rips through the bad, blasting through it once more.

Do this five times. Each time that first positive image shoots toward you, it ends bigger and brighter and the poor second image is gradually reduced until the last time, when it is completely destroyed.

Another technique to reduce or eliminate problems is through Tapping…

Tapping

"Human feelings are words expressed in human flesh. "

- Aristotle

This method has been demonstrated often by Paul McKenna on TV. It's safe and easy to do. Created by Dr Roger Callahan a psychologist trained in acupuncture, applied kinesiology and NLP, he devised Thought Field Therapy from insights from these three fields as a psychological version of acupuncture. Using a simple, painless procedure you tap on particular acupuncture points on your body so as you tap in the prescribed sequence, you distract your mind to reduce the unpleasant experience.

The procedure seems to access the meridian energy system where any emotions become trapped. The tapping creates vibrations in the energy system which appear to release the original energy disturbance and restores the even flow, somewhat like tapping on your central heating pipes to clear an air lock.

Unconvinced? Like many of the techniques in this manual, it seems strange at first, so is controversial, but it is based on scientific fact and has produced quick and substantial changes for many.

This process can reduce or eliminate any strong, defeatist feelings, beliefs, memories, emotions as it can physical symptoms.

While tapping, you must continue thinking about your problem throughout the whole sequence.

Close your eyes and think about your problem. Lets say you always play poorly on a slow, cracked pitch. You have painful accounts of unpredictable bounce and ducking short balls coming at your ribs. On a scale of 1-10, 1 being nothing and 10 being the worst it could ever be, where is your problem?

Still thinking about the problem pitch, take two fingers of either hand and tap firmly 10x above one of your eyebrows.

Now tap under that eye 10x.

Now tap 10x under your collar bone.

As you continue to think about your problem, tap under your armpit 10x.

Tap on the 'karate chop' side of your other hand.

Tap on the back of your other hand between the knuckles of your ring finger and little finger.

Open your eyes, then close them. Keep tapping. The following eye movements are connected to various brain functions.

Open your eyes. Look down to your right, then centre, then down to your left.

Keep tapping and as you do so, rotate your eyes 360 degrees anti-clockwise, then 360 degrees clockwise.

Still thinking about the slow pitch, hum the first few lines of happy birthday or a favourite tune. This humming allows switching between right brain hemisphere-left brain hemisphere-right brain hemisphere activity.

Next count aloud from 1-5.

Repeat the first few lines of happy birthday or your favourite tune.

Still thinking on the problem, close your eyes, tap 10x above your eye again.

Again tap under your collar bone.

Tap under your armpit.

Finally tap on the 'karate chop' point again.

Where is your problem regarding the slow pitch now on the scale of 1-10? You should have it down to a manageable level by the second go. If it hasn't reduced, go over the sequence again. It depends on how strong your problem was to start with, so it maybe need several attempts to reduce or completely eliminate it. Repeat as needed. You may get confused about what used to bother you.

Now I'll show you how the future can be your friend with Time Line...

Time Line

> *"If my mind can conceive it, and I can believe it, I then can achieve it."*
>
> - Larry Holmes

Part of you that's curious may wonder about this experience. Think of a time ahead when you can see yourself celebrating a success, how about Player of the Season, or holding aloft a trophy as captain while you celebrate with your team mates, the champagne corks popping, your supporters cheering. When you imagine that kind of future, your unconscious is directed toward making it happen.

Devised by Tad James, a Time Line is explained as an imaginary line where events happen and even where the unconscious stores memories. This line stretches off in one direction to your future and in the opposite direction for your past. Examples of this would be when you say 'I'm looking forward to seeing you' or 'I'll put this problem in the past.'

There are two parts to this exercise. First, how do you represent time? Think about something you do every day, if it's cricket related so much the better. As you see yourself doing this activity tomorrow, notice the direction you looked. Was your future in front, or was it to your left or right? Higher or lower? How far away?

Think about doing that task next week. Is the image further away, in front, behind, to the side. Higher or lower? Stay with me on this. What about a week ago in the past? Where were you doing the activity then?

Think about doing the same thing a month in the future. Is the image closer or further away? More in front or behind, more to one side or another. How about a month ago?

You can go on imagining the same activity three, six, twelve months in the future. Where is the picture?

Imagine all these pictures are dots joined together by a line as if you were connecting the dots inside your mind. This is how you unconsciously see time, your Time Line.

The second part of this exercise is creating your cricketing future, then live into it. Project yourself several months into your future, maybe the end of a rewarding season, see from your minds eye, out. Or maybe you have reached a goal. Everything has gone well, your game has improved, your more confident, your more knowledgeable. You have achievements in your life outside cricket.

Be curious about your future. Form an image of that ideal scene of everything you wish to happen in your future, It can be real or symbolic. See yourself there, happy and successful. Make the image big, bright, bold, richly colourful and anticipate how good you will feel the sparkle.

Now fill in the steps along the way to this ideal scene. Make a smaller image and place it a few weeks, or months, before this final big picture. Keep doing this until you have a succession of images connecting the present to your ideal future so that they get bigger each time, with good things happening along the way.

Look at those pictures you have created as stepping stones and imagine floating up out of your body and into each picture, spending a few moments living in each to absorb the positive experiences.

When you reach that final image, really get into the feeling of achievement as you discover yourself already there.

Finally return to the present and look along your future Time Line. Have confidence in the knowledge that it is a map for your unconscious to bring fulfilment to the future you have created.

Next, lets talk about Pain Control…

Pain Control

Pain means there is something wrong. If there is something wrong, you must find medical assistance.

No medical claims are expressed or implied here. Whatever the results you get, please continue to take any medication or actions prescribed by your health practitioner.

If you suffer pain or discomfort in any part of your body, just fifteen minutes of this exercise can make it disappear or diminish it significantly. Using the power of their mind, people who performed it were able to reduce pain by up to 80%.

A closed eye process is best, so learn the method first, or have someone read it to you. The purpose of this exercise is to look at the pain from a different perspective so you look beyond the pain. To your surprise you can get rid of it. Want it to happen, expect it to happen, allow it to happen. The power of your mind is powerful enough.

Get yourself relaxed somewhere you wont be disturbed. Without being cynical, without judging if you are doing it right, dismiss your rational mind and locate specifically the condition your suffering, now describe it.

How big is it? How long, thick, wide? What shape is it? A cube, flat, rectangle, round, square, triangle, is it jagged? Is it dull or sharp?

Just keep focusing on the condition. Describe exactly what it feels like. Pounding, pressing, pulsating, stretching, tearing?

Does it have a colour? A smell? A weight? If your not sure, just make it up.

Is there a temperature?

Now you have the location, shape and sensation of the condition, does it move?

Are you willing to let this condition go?

I want you to go inside your body and take it out. You can read that sentence again. Just imagine your reaching inside your body and taking the 'thing' out.

With your eyes still closed, imagine it in your hand. See the colour, the shape. Is it hard or can you mould it? Roll it up into a ball, go on, play with your condition. Toss it up into the air a few times and when your ready, throw it away saying 'goodbye' to it, or 'this no longer bothers me.' To your surprise you can get rid of it.

Now look inside. Are the symptoms still there? The same or changed? Lets focus on it a while longer.

How big is it now? What colour? Shape? Reach in and take it out of your body. How does that feel?

Hold it in your hand. Can you bend it? Drop it on the floor. Does it make a sound? Does it smash into pieces? Pick it up and roll it into a ball again. Tell yourself you no longer want it and hurl it away.

Is the condition still there? Know that you can do the process again. As you reduce the condition, mentally you get stronger.

Gently get centred back into your body and open your eyes.

You can also use that exercise on emotional issues of anger, grief or fear.

I'd like to introduce Noesitherapy-healing by thinking-and here credit the founder Dr Angel Escudero, a surgeon in Valencia. He has been investigated by medical experts who have praised his method, he has lectured to the medical world and he has been featured on a number of TV broadcasts around the globe. Dr Jonathan Royle who taught me this, uses Noesitherapy as part of his Complete Mind Therapy.

The theory behind Noesitherapy stems from the fight or flight response. Back in time, the caveman was constantly on full alert, especially out hunting. He would fight an opponent or an animal, but there would still be fear, so his mouth would go dry, muscles would tense and he would have extra strength due to the physiology of the body. When he defeated his foe or killed the animal, he would sigh with relief.

If he met an animal that wanted him for it's dinner, then flight would be the action. If he managed to get away, he sighed with relief and notice again his mouth was dry. That's the key. After any stress is over, saliva returns to the dry mouth. We also sigh and the muscles relax. I'll not get involved here with the other physical signs of heart beat, sweating, blood pressure, digestion, which is thousands of years conditioning in us humans, who now live in a different age. Just remember the saliva.

It's the apprehension, fear or expectancy of feeling pain that makes pain hurt or exist at all. You finish a DIY task and go to the sink to wash your hands and see blood. Nothing happened when the cut happened as your mind was somewhere else. The moment you see the blood, the cut starts stinging and funnily enough, bleeds more.

If your injured and your told you have to live with a certain amount of pain, then being able to reframe your mind so there's no pain, maybe just a little discomfort, makes it bearable.

Use the 1-10 scale to judge how much pain your experiencing.

Besides breathing deeply, your body is conditioned to relax with saliva. Use the idea of a lemon to get saliva working in your mouth. Lets suppose your right elbow is injured. Imagine your eating a tangy, juicy lemon, get the saliva on your tongue. This part is going to sound daft. Say to yourself aloud if you can, while the saliva is on your tongue 'my right elbow is now completely anaesthetized' which you say three times. The concept behind that is the first time the unconscious may ignore the conscious command as it's busy with other tasks. Ask a second time, the unconscious realises you are there and the third time the unconscious takes notice in a way that's right for you. Besides, Dr Escudero does it with his patients and he then carries out amputations.

Take a nice deep, relaxing breath. Imagine your right elbow has gone cold, it's like a lump of meat from a freezer. No discomfort to concern you. In a moment you can swallow the saliva, just say a few affirmations to yourself such as you feel no discomfort, you can turn off pain like a switch. Where is the pain now on the 1-10 scale?

If you feel pain or undue stiffness, get it looked at. Lets suppose you generally field on the boundary. You feel pain in your shoulder. Batting and bowling are ok, it's the throwing that causes the discomfort. But it's still a case of wanting to play and not let the side down even if you have a 'little niggle.' There you are with repetitive strain injury. All that throwing from the boundary has taken it's toll.

It's tough if you find yourself out through injury. You can do nothing, or use your time wisely. List the things you can do, perhaps studying DVD's, reading, cheer on your team mates. Perform any exercises you can do, even if its sat on an exercise bike with your arm in a sling.

Run videos in your head of doing well, which keep your mind focused and positive. Your mind stores what you have experienced and what you have thought the same way. This is perfect for mental training. You can train using visualisation to sharpen good technical and tactical techniques. The advantage is you can go through several repetitions of any technique in minutes without causing further injury.

No matter how confident you are, injuries do plant doubts in your mind which is why the mental side of recovery is so important. Now, it's important for me to make this next distinction for you- your not injured anymore! Your in a state of recuperation!

How about an injured opponent? Is it real or exaggerated? Ignore anything they say about their aches and pains. Assume it's for gamesmanship, sympathy or heroics. Give them no attention until after the match. If your opponent can stand on the field of play, they are healthy enough to warrant your best efforts. If their injury is real or not, it can have a negative influence on you.

Stay motivated with a cricket scrap book…

Cricket Scrap Book

> *"Peak performers from various fields maintain their childlike qualities!"*
>
> - Lars Eric Unestahl

Anyone wanting to invest time in cricket is advised to learn as much as they can about the sport. Read books, newspapers, magazines, watch films. Take clippings or photo-copies of pictures, diagrams and photos. Collect brochures of anything to bring into your cricketers life.

Every time you look at them, it reminds you of the goals yet to achieve, your role models, places you would like to play, equipment you would like to own. It keeps an account of your cricket activities, training logs, events, symbols, anything that gives you motivation and support.

Do the same with a video/DVD scrapbook. Watch the top players, study what works for them.

Use cricket bookmarks. Drink from a cricket mug. Dream in cricket bedding.

Keep larger items about your home or room that act as power-ful anchors. Look and handle them frequently. Use regular rehearsal time to smell the leather and feel the texture of the ball, swing the bat. Give yourself a sensory-rich experience. Concentration and rehearsal brings in countless nerve im-pulses.

Going slightly further, it may be helpful to concentrate on an object, a bat, ball, glove, even a poster on your wall. Study it while being relaxed. Use the exercise like a meditation session. When you notice your thoughts begin to wonder, return your full attention to your object. This exercise will improve your ability to focus and give you awareness of where your mind goes.

Get a picture of your hero in action, an exceptional keeper, a batsman of high quality owning a large range of strokes. Splice a photo of your head onto their body. Put it somewhere you can view it often. You may not posses all your hero's qualities, but your empowering your mind and stretching it beyond any limitations. Read the Mirroring chapter again, then copy and pretend until you become your own hero. Learn from the legends.

End of play is nearly upon us…

Conclusion

> *"Sports Psychology is the least studied of all cricket skills, even if it is widely accepted as being the most important ingredient of success. "*
>
> - Justin Langer

I'm out! There's not been a lot published on the psychological demands of cricket, I hope I have started a new trend. Being physically fit and technically adept is only part of being prepared these days. Mental and emotional strength are also required. I've covered mind techniques that can change your cricket, not just now, but progressively for years to come. This was written with Cricketers in mind, however many of the methods described are able to cross over into other areas of your life. As you become familiar with them, your energy and motivation will improve.

If you do nothing, what will happen? If you do something, what will happen?

We are all faced with opportunities disguised as impossible situations

Even a small change to your thinking can make a big difference. As you continue with the new way, you'll begin to realise how much you've changed. Don't look how far you have to go, rather how far you have come. As you have learnt, the conscious mind can only think of one thing at a time, why not make it something positive. You can, can you not?

You should make this manual important enough to return to it several times to get the results you need. Why not carry it around in your kit bag. No single technique is a magic pill, but when you practice them repeatedly, they will become familiar. You can even go to the beginning and start reading again.

When I was learning to drive I practised again and again until I was confident enough to pass my test, just as drivers before me have done. All I needed was the confidence practice would bring. I didn't presume driving wouldn't work on my first attempt. Please keep that in mind. If a method doesn't work on your first attempt, don't give up on it. Understand these tried and tested techniques do work. They work beautifully. You may even find one an exciting and rewarding activity.

Imagine staring into a mirror after a match and honestly telling the person you see there, you've done your best. Feeling the pride and joy of a perfect performance. The delight you have created for your team mates, the fans, the directors, your coach and your mind coach-sorry about that blatant 'sales plug.'

I sincerely hope you enjoy what's presented here and I really want you to succeed, because by your success this manual will be judged. Have fun and enjoy your Cricket.

Some suggestions were indirect, embedded into the text to place them into your unconscious mind.

The time to start using them is now…

Bibliography

Andrew, Keith., The Skills of Cricket.

Bolstad, Dr Richard., Resolve.

Callahan, Dr Roger., Tapping the Healer Within.

Court, Martyn., The Winning Mindset.

Eason, Adam., The Secrets of Self-Hypnosis.

Edgette, John H & Rowan, Tim., Winning the Mind Game.

Hodgson, David., The Buzz.

Hughes, Simon., Jargonbusting: Mastering the Art of Cricket.

Mack, Garry with David Casstevens., Mind Gym.

McKenna, Paul., Change Your Life in Seven Days.

Mycoe, Stephen., Unlimited Sports Success.

Robbins, Anthony., Awaken the Giant Within.

Robbins Blair, Forbes., Instant Self-Hypnosis.

Royle, Dr Jonathan., Confessions of a Hypnotist.

Waterfield, Robin., Hidden Depths.

Self Hypnosis for Cricket

Introduction

Lets take it one easy step at a time. To begin, there are many myths about hypnosis, often undeserved which I should clear up. It's not magical, nor does it give someone magic powers. Nor can it turn you into superman otherwise we would all be flying around. You cannot get 'stuck' in hypnosis, you do not put yourself under someone else's power who will then take control of you. You cannot become possessed. You cannot be made to do something which is against your moral code. You do not leave your body, you do not lose your mind.

Let me reassure you, hypnosis is a natural state of mind which can be used as an efficient psychological tool for a Cricketer to reach full potential.

Those easiest to hypnotise have the strongest, most creative minds with the greatest ability to use their intelligence. Very few people are not able to get into a hypnotic state and there is usually a reason. Epilepsy can create difficulty to focus, the really mentally subnormal, senility and alcohol or drug abuse.

The media thrives on drama and many stories in books and on film are the child of fertile imaginations, who use the evil hypnotist to heighten the tension. Those authors themselves have probably been influenced by another authors mistaken idea of what hypnosis is about.

Most of the misunderstandings come from stage shows where the participants are in full agreement to the suggestions they have been given. Those people on stage are volunteers who are fully prepared to go along with the entertainment. And that's all it is, entertainment.

With Clinical Hypnosis, I am not going to get you to bark like a dog, that's not going to cure your bowling problem or help you achieve your innings goal. Hypnosis is a reliable, therapeutic method recognised by orthodox medicine.

Here you will discover how to help yourself achieve success in Cricket. Surprisingly you have been in hypnosis many times before, although you may not realise it. A regular journey, to work for example, when you realise you don't remember getting there. Don't worry about anything like that though, your unconscious is on constant duty making sure you are safe. As soon as conscious attention is needed, your unconscious gets you there instantly.

How about reading when you realise you haven't noticed a single word because your mind has been some place else. Or your watching a film and you don't realise someone is talking to you until they start shouting to get your attention, because you have been absorbed with the story on the screen.

These are all forms of hypnosis which happen to you everyday. The examples show you were focused, however on something else.

Some clients think they failed to 'go under' as nothing more than extreme relaxation took place. They knew they could move or open their eyes if they wanted to, they were just too comfortable to be bothered. That's what hypnosis can be for some people. The best way to describe what you may experience, is remember how you feel just moments before actual sleep occurs, or moments before you wake up. At that moment you pass through a state very similar to hypnosis.

Here are some of the sensations you may experience, it's different for everybody:

> Extremely relaxed
> Floaty
> Tingling in your hands or features
> Feeling either light or heavy
> More awareness, senses heightened
> Warmth or cold
> Stress free

Preparation

I'm going to teach you a preparation routine which I would like you to practise. Do it with your eyes open a few times so you can read yourself through it, it's easy to remember.

Make sure you wont be disturbed for about ten minutes and visit the toilet before you begin. Sit comfortably. Some people prefer a straight-backed chair to an armchair. Have both your feet flat on the floor and your hands are relaxed in your lap.

Exercise

Close your eyes and imagine a feeling of ease and peace drifting down through your body relaxing every muscle. If you find that difficult, imagine how it would feel if your muscles were relaxed. Slow your breathing right down so that your breathing so gently, you wouldn't disturb a feather placed near your nose.

Don't rush it. Relaxation comes in it's own time. After a while, you'll feel yourself bcoming calmer, quieter, your mind as still as your body. It's even fine if you notice your more aware than ever before. Stay with it.

And open your eyes when your ready.

How was that? You can actually go into hypnosis with that simple routine. You may have been surprised at just how easy images can form.

Visualisation

You should practice and become good at visualisation as it will lead you to success in your aims and goals. Some people think they can't visualise anything as they can't 'see' pictures in their minds eye. You don't have to see something exactly as if you were looking at a photograph. Try this. Remember a short journey you did today. Something as simple as going from your front door to your living room. Imagine in your mind starting out and finishing it. Whatever it was, that's a visualisation for you.

Effective visualisation practice should use more of your senses than visual imagery. This way your other senses can be strengthened. Imagine what coffee smells like? How about freshly cut grass? Can you hear a whistle or crowd applause? What does your hair feel like? Don't touch it, imagine it. You may be more aware of another sense than vision.

Once you get used to it, you'll soon be able to imagine every smell you can think of, any sound you have ever heard, any texture you have felt. Practice, smell things, feel things, listen to sounds.

Exercise

This time, find somewhere comfortable to sit where you wont be disturbed for twenty minutes or so. Put to one side any problems you are having to deal with, they'll still be there when you come back. In fact, after some mental work, you may be able to deal with them more efficiently. One easy trick is to visualise a box or even a kit bag where you can place all your mental and emotional difficulties until you have time to sort them out.

Go through the preperation routine as before and when you are ready, recall some ordinary event that's happened in the last day or so. Remember your senses. How did it look? How did it sound? How did it feel? How did it smell or taste?

With practice, your memories will become more detailed. These images, when used in hypnosis, provide an edge to creating maximum success as you shall see.

Let's get into self-hypnosis.

Self-Hypnosis

You should now be comfortable with the preperation and visual routines as I'm going to explain to you a three-part routine for getting into the hypnotic state.

But first, how do you come out of self-hypnosis? Simply finish the session by telling yourself to do so. Tell yourself you will be wide awake and alert, feeling fine on the count of five, then count yourself up from one to five and opening your eyes. Practice that a few times.

Part 1

Close your eyes. Bring to mind a special day that you have had, even a great day out. Notice how the memory starts, remember it and store it in your mind, you will use it later. Bring all your senses in now, remembering what you saw, what you heard, what you felt, even what you smelt and tasted if they are relevant.

Make everything real in your mind and keep focused until you can almost re-live one or more of those senses. It will often be the visual one, but don't let it concern you if you don't get it exact, it takes practice. As long as you have an awareness something is there is fine enough. Allow it to happen rather than force it happen.

Part 2

With your eyes closed, imagine you are breathing peace into every cell of your body, each and every fibre of your being. And with every exhalation, you are letting go of any tension. Let each and every muscle from your head to your toes go limp as you exhale and repeat the word 'relax.' After half a dozen or so breaths, let yourself imagine you are drifting further down and you are becoming more relaxed, more than you have ever been. If you feel yourself floating up, just go with that.

Part 3

Remember in Part 1 storing the memory of a perfect day? You can use that now as a trigger for getting into self-hypnosis. This is best achieved after getting some practice with the first two parts. To use this trigger is very simple. After doing the preperation routine (it gets easier and faster the more you practice) and once your settled using Part 2, bring your happy memory to mind and let it help you drift down into trance-it's that easy.

When your ready, count yourself out.

I or You

There are countless ways to achieve self-hypnosis, the method I have shown you is just one. When your in, read a prepared script or use a tape recorder to give yourself your desires. It's best to work on one thing at a time.

It's usual for people to say 'I will,' 'I can,' 'I'm going to.' This may be fine for you, but some people respond better by being told what to do, such as 'you will,' 'you can,' 'your going to.' It doesn't matter what you use, 'I' or 'you', as long as you use the form that feels right for you. If your unsure, make a script or recording using both versions to see which one you better respond to, just don't mix the two up together.

Reading a script is as good as making a recording once you get yourself into hypnosis. Have you ever been so absorbed in a book you lost all sense of time? Someone spoke to you and you didn't notice them? That's hypnosis. Once your in hypnosis just tell yourself you will open your eyes and start reading following Part 3, read, then at the end of the script, close your eyes ready to count yourself up. For either script or recording, you may enjoy some quiet relaxation music playing in the background.

Now I'll show you how to use the state of hypnosis to achieve mastery.

Uses

Lets look how to actually use self-hypnosis to achieve your goals and desires.

Be sure your now used to getting into and out of hypnosis, if your not, your efforts will be wasted. I can't repeat this enough, you must have a full grasp how to do it. The direct suggestions you will give yourself have to be compounded, so practice until it's so ingrained it will be an automatic response.

You will always be aware of sounds as your not asleep, so simply relax. So if anything noisy happens outside, your covered. Any sound you hear will not affect or disturb you, in fact, you can actually use any sound to deepen the trance. If there is heavy traffic outside, just tell yourself that all the traffic noise will help you to be more comfortable, deeper relaxed.

Caution
At the start of the session always tell yourself you will awake immediately if your full attention is needed for any emergency situation as a safety device. A further caution is not to drive or operate any machinery during your self-hypnosis session as it can slow down reflexes.

You can feel better, change habits, learn, block pain and so much more. Just decide what goal you need. For setting your goals, there are four 'must' rules which apply to every goal;

Plausible & Realistic
You nor I are magicians. If you are seventy years old you will not play for the Ashes. If it's not

possible without hypnosis, it's not possible with. If you can't vary the flight and pace of your deliveries, then hypnosis won't create mastery instantly for you, however, hypnosis can get you to the highest standard possible for you to produce those deliveries.

Suitable for Personality

For your goal to succeed, it should reflect your personality. Although hypnosis allows people to behave in a way which is different from their 'norm', that's only temporary, so is no good for long- term goals. Select a goal which would not surprise a family member that you were doing it, then use hypnosis to speed up the process and become proficient at it.

Make it Clear

You need to know what it is that you want. Many people say 'I want to be a winner.' Ok, a winner at what? Your unconscious has the mind of a seven year old, it works only with uncomplicated, simple statements, not ambiguous ones. 'I want to average at least one century every season' is a clear goal. That is achievable.

Make it Positive

Think of what you want, not what you don't want. What you can do, not what you can't. What you like, not what you don't like. 'I don't cover my off stump enough' is not a positive statement. 'I want to cover my off stump competently' is. By implication, consciously they mean the same to you, but the literal meaning unconscious does not understand implications. 'I am determined not to be bowled out' is a negative statement. 'I am determined to protect my wickets' carries a different message to your unconscious, which can only function on what IS, not understanding what IS NOT.

The Four Senses Test

You should apply at least four of your senses to your visualisation of any goal. You should SEE yourself doing it successfully, receiving a reward perhaps; HEAR something associated with it, applause maybe; FEEL something associated, how about the cool metal of that trophy in your hands and then SMELL or TASTE something there, celebratory champagne for example.

Now turn all that into a living video, make it a rich, sense filled experience you can go over and over in your mind. As you practice using your senses, you will expan your conscious awareness.

It's best to work on one goal at a time, each goal can run into the next as you progress. Working on one goal at a time makes it more likely for you to achieve it and is a lot easier than trying to remember a jumble of scenarios.

Get yourself into hypnosis and be patient, you can't hurry it. Once there, play your video in your mind three, four, five times and let yourself feel the excitement of this adventure each time. That's an emotional reward for yourself and is an important part of the success plan, so make it your reality.

Each time you do self-hypnosis, you'll do it better than the time before. Want it to happen, let it happen.

You now have the skills to improve your Cricket.

Did you enjoy that?

Conclusion

That's all there is to it. There is far, far more to the art of hypnosis than I have covered here. There are many books, DVD's, courses on this fascinating subject and it's always good to compare more than one person's spin on the subject.

Feel free to email me, I'll do my best to answer, although my workload of therapy, writing, coaching and so on keeps me busy. Eventually I will get back to you. My email address is mind4@merseymail.com

Enjoy your Cricket

Notes

About the Author

Always being involved in sport, Paul Maher started his career in the health & fitness industry over twenty years ago as a Health Club Manager and Trainer. An interest in sport injuries found him studying for a diploma in Sport Therapy and he also improved his qualifications becoming an Excercise Professional Advanced Instructor Level Three.

Aware of the limited mindset some injured athletes endure, besides motivating others, Paul began to study Sport Psychology, however it is Hypnosis which fuelled his enthusiasm to help the public as well as those involved in sport.

Lightning Source UK Ltd.
Milton Keynes UK
18 November 2009

146408UK00001B/20/P